The Mindful Mother's Way

the

mindful

mother's
way

....

FINDING CONFIDENCE,
CONNECTION, AND CALM IN
THE PRACTICE OF MOTHERHOOD

....

SARAH GYAMPOH

Kat Biggie Press
Columbia, SC 29229

The Mindful Mother's Way is published by Kat Biggie Press
http://katbiggiepress.com

Cover design by Michelle Fairbanks, Fresh Design
Editing by Liz Thompson, House Style Editing
Interior design by Write|Publish|Sell

ISBN-13: 978-1-948604-08-6
Library of Congress Control Number: 2018906792
First Edition: June 2018

10 9 8 7 6 5 4 3 2 1

Contents

Part 3

Dedication

In memory of my mom,
Debbie Shapiro 5/8/53 - 6/25/98

Acknowledgments

What an incredible journey it has been writing this book, and I couldn't have done it alone. First and foremost, I would like to thank all my female ancestors whose lives made mine a possibility, especially my mom. I love you so much, and I'm grateful for our eternal connection. I know you are celebrating with me.

To my children, Dreidan, Ariav, Ezra, and Nhyira, for choosing me to be your mother, and for being my best teachers. You fill my heart with an abundance of love, and it's a true honor to call myself your mom.

For Harvey and Joe Shapiro, the best dad and brother a girl could ask for, thank you for loving me even when I was at my most unlovable.

To my husband, Kwame, for your love, your belief in me, and the way you encourage me to keep going even when I am ready to quit. Odo nkate cake.

For my sister-friends, Amanda, Angela, Audrey, Aviva, Carlee, Courtney, Elissa, Fara, Heather, Jacque, Janelle, Julia, Kristin, Nets, Pam, Talia, and Teri. I love you. You've all supported me in ways you may not be aware of, and I am ever grateful for the friendship I share with each of you.

To the Sunday Mastermind group, thanks for supporting me in every step of the journey, and for not rolling your eyes at me when I decided to change the title and subtitle for the 400th time. Your love, activism, missions, and dreams inspire me.

Mike Hill, Kylie Slavik, and the students in the Conscious Marketing Academy, thank you for helping me find and define my voice and vision, and for the encouragement and know-how to share my story. Your insight and wisdom helped me transform from victim to victor, and for that, I will always be thankful.

To every mom and caregiver that is showing up daily to mother and nurture children, thank you. Your dedication is what will make this world a better place, and I am happy to be walking the path of motherhood with you.

For the power trio, Alexa, Liz, and Michelle, thank

you for helping me to birth and beautify *The Mindful Mother's Way.* I couldn't have done it without you.

And last, but not least, thank you to the universe, G-d[1], the divine, nature, and the magic that conspired to support me in this venture. The signs I received along the way helped me to keep going and know this was meant to come from me. I am honored you chose me, and I hope I did it justice.

Walking the Path of Motherhood

On June 11th, 2007, I sat in my friend Sam's bathroom staring at the little pink plus sign in the pregnancy test window, knowing my life was about to change in a major way. I had recently finished service with the Peace Corps in the Dominican Republic, and I was in my first year of graduate school studying to become a Social Worker. I always wanted to have children, but having a baby while still in school wasn't part of my plan. I could hear my Grandma's voice running through my mind saying, "We make plans and G-d laughs."

When the thoughts in my mind finally calmed, and I was able to leave the bathroom, I shared the

---

1 Note: It is customary in Judaism to *not* write the name of G-d in a place where it may be discarded or erased.

news with Sam, and she gave me a giant hug and congratulated me. The fact that I was pregnant was starting to sink in now, and I was both nervous and excited. I called my partner, and he was also thrilled. This was really happening. I was going to have a baby. Someone was going to call me mom.

I started reading everything I could get my hands on about pregnancy and the fetus's development. I went to my prenatal appointments eager to learn as much as I could from the midwife. Hearing the heartbeat for the first time was the greatest sound in the world. Those whooshes of the heart pumping blood were like pure magic to my ears.

Being pregnant was very sacred to me, and made me feel more connected to everything in the universe. The colors of the flowers blooming in springtime seemed more vibrant, and the love I felt inside of me was the strongest I had ever experienced. The only thing missing from my life was my mom, and I wished she was around to share this special time with me. Now I understood why she fought her illness for so long, for her children.

I was awakened in the early morning hours of February 3rd, 2008, in labor. Although I felt nervous about giving birth, labor went smoothly, and in the afternoon on February 4th, I held my son in my arms for the first time. I was so overcome with emotion, feeling happy, sad, nervous, filled with love, and tired all rolled into one intense emotional experience. Staring at his perfect little face made me want to be the best mom and person I could be.

Caring for my son was truly amazing as I enjoyed experiencing life through his eyes. His laugh and smile could melt away any stress I was feeling and take me out of the thoughts in my head to the present moment. Because my professors were understanding and flexible, I was fortunate to be able to finish grad school and graduate with my class. And, although I had planned to go to work upon graduating, the birth of my son changed that. I wanted to be home with him, soaking in every ounce of his being and learning about the beauty of the world through his eyes, and that is what I did. I was in pure bliss, until I wasn't.

One evening when my partner returned from work, I remember looking at him with the death stare. "I need you to take the baby, so I can shower, get something to eat, and have a minute to breathe," were the words I greeted him with. My son was having a colicky day, and I hadn't had a minute to myself all day. I was drowning, and I needed him to take the baby so that I could come up for air.

In taking care of my son, I had buried my needs, and on that day, I realized that I needed to start caring for myself again. I got back onto my yoga mat and looked into becoming an instructor. I found a training that would begin in a few months when my son was 6-months-old, and I decided to enroll.

Yoga teacher training, like motherhood, revealed more of who I was. I connected with parts of my being I had forgotten were there. My yoga mat became a refuge for me. A place where I could go when the challenges of motherhood were overwhelming me, and I needed a space to just be. During the graduation ceremony, my son took some of his earliest steps, and it was beautiful to see how we were both growing, evolving, and developing.

We decided we wanted to have more children, and we had three more. Our older three are boys, and the youngest is a girl. Mothering four children brings me great joy, and it can also be overwhelming at times. I can go from martyr-mommy to mommy-monster at the drop of a hat, and I knew something had to change.

"Don't do that!" "I need a minute to breathe!" "Stop hitting each other!" I was yelling more than I care to admit, and sometimes fantasized about getting in the van, driving away, and never looking back.

I was drowning, and my mistake was not confiding

in anyone, and even denying it to myself. I convinced myself, or maybe society convinced me, that "good moms" do it all and don't ask for help. "Good moms" don't feel like they aren't doing or being enough, and they certainly never feel guilty if they want to take time to care for themselves. Admitting you need help makes you weak and shows you are incapable.

My pride got in the way of me asking for and admitting to myself that I needed help, which resulted in waking one morning to my world spinning out of control. I confided in my husband, and he stepped in and made breakfast for the children so I could rest. I relaxed on the couch, and the first thought that came to mind was that maybe I was pregnant, although it was unlikely. After resting for a while, I sat up to nurse my daughter and once again the room started to spin. I nursed her, drank a tall glass of water, and took a nap hoping to feel better. It didn't work. After the nap, I still felt horrible.

My daughter needed to nurse again, and since she was playing on the ground, I decided to lay next to her and nurse her. When I tried to get up, the spinning became even more intense, and I began to cry. I was terrified. I had no clue what was happening, and all I could think about was my four young children and how much they needed me. I told my husband that I should go to the hospital and we decided it would be best for him to call an ambulance.

Upon arrival at the hospital, I was examined, and the doctor diagnosed me with vertigo. I was released from the hospital after a few hours, and, once home, slept as much as I could for the next few days.

When I was finally feeling better, I began to restructure my daily routine. I knew I had to adjust my expectations and make time for the self-care I so desperately needed. Today, my days look different. I wake up before anyone else and take time to meditate, read, work, practice yoga, and care for myself. I fill my cup, so I have plenty to give to my children.

I no longer carry the weight of the world on my shoulders. I treasure the little things—the flowers given to me by my 5-year-old every time we go for a walk, the living room dance parties, and all the moments spent playing with my children. When I'm feeling stressed, and I can feel the mommy-monster wanting to make an appearance, I take a deep breath or walk away from the situation. It's not always possible to avoid yelling, but I've learned to accept this part of my being and not feel ashamed for having an intense emotional experience.

I've learned to slow down, do what I can, and let everything else go. The laundry pile can wait. That being present is vital. We are all perfectly imperfect, and when my children push my buttons, I thank them for showing me the parts of my being that still need healing. Life is happening now, and these are the times to enjoy.

At first, I thought my circumstances were rare, but I quickly found that I was not alone. We are on this path of motherhood together, and when one of us finds peace, we all feel it. As we heal, the collective heals, and it begins with the self. My mission in life now is to pass on the lessons I have learned, the techniques I've been shown, and to help other moms find acceptance, connect with their truth, and their maternal essence— the part of you that is pure love and holds all the answers you seek.

This book is my offering to you, precious mother, and I hope it helps you awaken your innate wisdom, deepens the bond you have with your children, and reminds you to celebrate YOU.

So much love,

Introduction

*T*he *Mindful Mother's Way* is an invitation to make small shifts in your daily life, creating time and space for nurturing, knowing, embracing, and being yourself. In doing so, you will invite more mindfulness, presence, joy, play, and love into your day. Its foundation is built upon the belief that motherhood helps you to find yourself, and is both a practice and spiritual journey. It is an exploration of the concept and a practical guide to the power of practicing mindfulness and savoring the extraordinary in the ordinary. My hope is that in your times of calmness, you strengthen your spiritual core, connect with your innate wisdom and how you choose to mother, and find ways to celebrate motherhood's journey. After all, the days are long but the years are short.

This book can be used in many ways, and you choose how it works best for you. It can serve as a meditation guide, a daily reminder, a go-to for answers, and even as a friend when you are having one of "those days." Part 1 explores the what and why of mindfulness and how incorporating it into your life can enrich your life and mothering. Part 2 consists of anecdotes and practices designed to help you restore calm, increase confidence, be present with and release strong emotions, and deepen the connection with yourself and your children. Part 3 is a celebration of you and the mother you are.

While writing this book, I was given plenty of opportunities daily to put the principles to work. Trying to find calm when my boys are treating the living room like a wrestling arena and peace when their play turns into physical fighting. Some days, I was more successful than others, and on the days when I felt like I just couldn't win, I gave myself some grace and reminded myself of my humanity and my perfect imperfection. Sometimes this is easier said than done, and I am grateful for apologies, second chances, and hugs.

There are times when I look at my children, and my

heart fills with love and tears of joy stream down my face. I feel incredibly blessed to witness their growth and becoming who they are. They make me want to be the best version of myself, and always try again when I feel I've let them down. It's all part of the process.

Yes, the days are long on this path of motherhood. And some days seem to never end, when the children are in break-down mode and needing me to assist them with all of their daily tasks. These times of overwhelm are when I call on my highest self to remind myself to slow down, take a deep breath, and do what I can. The lotus comes from the murkiest water, just as motherhood's challenges allow us to grow into the best version of ourselves.

Before we are mothers, we are individuals, and that is why many of the practices are designed to be completed alone. To give our children respect, acceptance, encouragement, boundaries, and above all unconditional love, we have to learn and practice them with ourselves. The relationship we have with ourselves is the most valuable relationship, as it sets the tone for all our other relationships.

The way we mother is as unique as our fingerprints. When we are able to quiet down, seek within and connect with our maternal essence, we always choose what's right for our children and for us as we will never lead ourselves astray. We have all the answers we need available to us at all times.

The Mindful Mother's Way will help you find the space between the thoughts, before the reaction, which is your truth. You will be guided on the path which leads you back home to yourself. There is no perfect here, only perfect imperfection and love.

Mindful Mother's Manifesto

I am a mother. Within me, I hold all of the beauty and wonder of life, being alive, and the universe. I understand and embrace every aspect of my being. I practice presence and release myself from perfection. I care for my body, mind, and spirit. I play to feed my soul and enjoy my children. I laugh. I cry. I hug. I kiss. I heal. I honor myself and my children. I move my body to shift energy and release strong emotions when needed. I prepare food with love and fuel my body with whole foods. I recognize the wisdom I carry within. This is my motherhood. I am a mindful mother.

Chapter 1

What Is Mindfulness and
How Can We Apply the Practice to
Motherhood?

Mindfulness is being conscious of and paying attention to the current moment where life is happening. It's noticing your experience with open-hearted, non-judgmental awareness, no matter the situation. When we incorporate mindfulness practices into our daily lives, we notice our reality begins to shift. So simple, yet it requires effort to quiet the mind and focus on the now.

Our minds are continually processing numerous things at the same time, especially in modern times, we tend to multi-task—washing dishes while talking on the phone and simultaneously having a conversation with someone standing next to us. We carry around long to-do lists, and always have somewhere to go and something to do.

I am certainly guilty of trying to do it all at once. Half-playing with my children while responding to an email on my phone, and doing a poor job at both.

While this is the norm, it doesn't have to be your reality. Mindfulness can be easily interwoven into your life and can be practiced at any time, even while folding laundry or waiting in the car line to pick up your children from school. Like our breath, mindfulness is an ever-present friend waiting to be called on and put to use.

When my oldest was a newborn, a well-meaning friend gifted me a book that had a way to decipher your baby's cries to figure out the reason for the crying. I studied the book, listened to the CD, and felt prepared to put the information to use. "Neh," meant the baby is hungry, "Owh," baby is sleepy, "Heh," baby is uncomfortable, "Eairh," baby has gas, and "Eh," baby needs to be burped.

One day when my son was crying, I decided to give it a try. I listened to his cry and tried to figure out what he was communicating. After about a minute passed, which seemed like a lifetime listening to him cry, I scrapped the listening idea and picked him up. I realized I didn't have magical ears that could distinguish the noises he was making, but I could pick him up and comfort him.

The way you experience and incorporate mindfulness into your life will be in the way that is right for you. I suggest framing your day with some of the practices that are explained in the first three pillars I've outlined in the book. As an example, begin your day expressing gratitude for a new day, and quiet your mind before your feet touch the ground. End your day with writing in your journal or practicing the mudra, hand gesture, for a good morning. You will discover what feels good for you and may even create your own rituals.

When we pay attention to the now, we are present in our lives, emotions, and for those around us. As moms, mindfulness serves us well as our children are always seeking our attention and recognition, and when we can "be" with them, we notice our relationship changing and becoming more intimate.

There are four main pillars that I created, serving as the key components to practicing mindful motherhood: sacred being, open-hearted relationships, magical movements, and food for the soul. You will see I've categorized the anecdotes and practices using these pillars as guides, always choosing the one which is more predominant when there were two or more possibilities.

Sacred Being

Sacred being refers to connecting with and expressing who we are at the core level, our soul or being. These practices allow us to access our inner essence, love in its purest form, by removing all the veils that keep us from it.

Open-Hearted Relationships

Open-hearted relationships are those that honor and respect all parties involved. The freedom to express all of our emotions is integral to having an open-hearted relationship. In these sacred relationships, we acknowledge our humanity, and that of our children, and accept it all as part of the whole.

The practices within this section are about the relationship we have with our children. They allow us to deepen the bond with them and open our hearts to all the love we can give and receive.

Magical Movements

Magical movements are sacred and enable us to harness ancient wisdom by placing our body in certain postures or positions that allow us to achieve a desired outcome, such as increased happiness, or drawing energy to keep up with our children. As always, honor your body when practicing these movements. If something doesn't feel right, modify the movement or don't do it. There is no force involved in these practices. Be gentle with yourself and allow your body to guide you.

Food for the Soul

Our bodies are wise, and if we listen to what they say, we will be able to nourish ourselves accordingly. Sugar addiction, eating processed foods, and being stressed out, all contribute to dulling the messages and making it harder to recognize which foods our body is requesting.

Slowing down, simplifying, and preparing and eating real food, are all vital to nourishing our bodies mindfully. When we connect with our body and hear the messages it sends, we eat what we need, no more and no less.

We aim to eat the plant, not the food made in a plant. Eating foods that are in their natural state not only provides us with more energy, it also helps our minds stay clear, and aids in balancing our hormones and emotions. Sit and enjoy your meal whenever possible.

Chapter 2

The Science of Our Nervous System

*A*s mothers, we are often in the middle of one task when we are called to do another, and we barely have time to catch our breath in between. We go from task to task hastily moving throughout the day. Wake up, make breakfast, feed children, wash dishes, brush teeth (your own and the children's), wash faces, get dressed and the list goes on . . . and all of this usually happens before 8 a.m.

In all of this busyness, it's no wonder that we get stressed out and rarely have time to catch our breath, let alone take a deep breath. Our brains are not wired to multi-task, but rather mono-task, and functioning in this "putting out fires" mode elicits a physiological response similar to what would occur if we were being chased by a bear. The autonomic nervous system is in charge of how we cope with any given situation. When we feel threatened, our fight-or-flight response is set into action when an alarm goes off in the amygdala, an almond-shaped region of the brain, and cortisol and adrenaline are released.

Our body responds by activating the sympathetic nervous system and increasing our heart rate, our muscles are provided extra blood, our breathing quickens, and our blood sugar spikes, all providing more fuel for the brain to react and the body to move—great if you need to escape that hungry bear, not so awesome if you need to change a diaper and realize your dog just threw up in the living room.

While some stress can be beneficial, in that it excites us and allows us to put our all into something, living with chronic stress is not ideal. It leads to high blood pressure and sugar, inflammation, poor digestion, difficulty concentrating, and more appearances of the good old "mommy monster." You know, the being that takes over your body when you lose it.

When we are stressed and functioning in fight-

or-flight mode controlled by the highly reactive amygdala, we often say or do things we may regret later. We are quick to want to put out the fire, and that may lead to undesired behavior. I call this the overreacting and guilt cycle. We lose our cool, feel bad about it, and then "punish" ourselves for having lost our cool. Holding ourselves in shame keeps us in the past and doesn't allow us to move past the experience.

If we can pause for a second, and stop the amygdala from setting things into motion and take a deep breath, the prefrontal cortex, a more rational part of the brain, kicks in and we move from overwhelm to "I got this" and can respond rather than react. The problem is that most times this is easier said than done unless we have a practice in place to take ourselves out of the reactive mode. When we are able to stop the reaction, the parasympathetic nervous system is activated, and we are more level-headed.

The rest and digest system is responsible for controlling homeostasis, or the balance and maintenance of the body's functions. It restores the body to a state of calm and allows it to relax and repair. Your saliva production increases, digestive enzymes are released, your heart rate lowers, the bronchial tubes in your lungs constrict, your muscles relax, the pupils constrict, and you urinate more frequently. All of these changes are designed to maintain long-term health, improve digestion, conserve energy, and maintain a healthy balance in your body.

Breaking free from fight-or-flight and reducing stress as often as possible is ideal. Our bodies prefer to function in rest and digest mode, and the more frequently we do it, the easier it becomes to do as we strengthen those neural pathways. One deep breath at a time.

Adding mindfulness practices to your day will allow you to find your center and lessen your stress and anxiety. You'll experience less fight-or-flight reactiveness, and find yourself staying in rest and digest more.

Chapter 3

The Tools We Use in Mindful Motherhood

To best deal with life and mothering challenges, it benefits us to discover and trust the innate wisdom we all possess—our maternal essence. When we can live from this place of our being, our challenges are easier to manage because we are living and mothering our way, honoring our truth.

Building a strong core and connecting to our maternal essence, allows us to be and accept who we are at the soul level, pure love paired with our perfect imperfection.

In the busyness of our modern lives, we often

ignore our intuition or are too busy going, going, going to have the time and space to listen to and honor it. There are some practices outlined in the next chapter, but first, an explanation of what they are and why we do them.

Meditation

Meditation is the state of being present with a quiet mind to achieve emotional calmness. There are many meditative techniques such as focusing on your breath, focusing on an object, walking meditation, guided meditation and others.

I've found the simplest way to practice meditation is to focus on your breathing. Find a comfortable place to sit and begin to notice the natural rhythm of your breath. Inhale and exhale slowly through your nose, lengthening your breath.

Concentrate on your breath and allow the awareness of your breath to bring you to a meditative state where your mind is quiet, and your body is relaxed. When thoughts arise, allow them to float by without engaging them. If you are drawn to a thought, no problem, bring your concentration back to your breathing, and you will return to the state of meditation.

Practicing meditation is beneficial to our well-being in many ways. It increases our ability to focus, not only while we are practicing, but when we aren't practicing as well. We experience less anxiety, we are more creative, we express more compassion for others, our memory improves, our level of stress decreases, and the amount of gray matter in our brain increases. All of these benefits lead to more positive emotions, heightened focus, and emotional stability. Meditation has also been shown to reduce the decline of our cognitive functioning by diminishing the age-related effects on our gray matter.

Overall, meditation is a practice that can be done by anyone with the desire to do so. While there are many techniques, focusing on your breath is a great way to get started.

Japa Meditation is a particular type of meditation where a mala, traditionally a necklace with 108 beads, is used to count repetitions of a mantra. By reciting the mantra, either aloud, as a whisper, or holding it at your third eye, you calm your mind, focus your energy, and can reach a deeper meditative state.

Breath Work

Focusing on our breath and controlling how we

breathe is an extremely powerful way to alter our state of being. It is said that a single conscious breath is a meditation. Our breath chooses how we want our body to feel.

Pranayama is the formal practice of controlling the breath, which is the source of our prana or vital life force.

Whenever we desire, we can shift our reality by focusing on and changing our breathing. Some of my best breath work happens when I am in line at the grocery store or caught in traffic.

We can use our breath to calm and invigorate ourselves. Also, if we can take a full deep breath before reacting to a situation, it gives us the opportunity to find balance and respond in a more balanced way.

Mudra

Mudras are hand gestures that allow us to tap into and harness our innate wisdom and power. They are the keys to revealing your unseen power, the most sacred of all.

Historically, we can trace the use of hand gestures as a language all the way back to the ancient Egyptians. These sacred hand gestures were used by high priests and priestesses to communicate with the gods, manifest miracles, and connect with the afterlife.

Egyptians carved these gestures on the walls of and inside the pyramids, and they became the base of their hieroglyphs. From Egypt, these movements and the knowledge of their spiritual power and usage spread to India and Greece.

In India, they were named mudras, a Sanskrit word, meaning "seal," "mark," or "gesture," a symbolic or ritual gesture in Hinduism and Buddhism. While some mudras involve the entire body, most are performed with the hands and fingers.

Plato shared the gestures in Greece where they were categorized as being either comic, tragic, or satiric. From Egypt and Greece, the gestures were brought to Rome, which is how they became a part of popular discourse and culture.

Emperor Augustus of Rome delighted in viewing the performances of hand gestures in pantomimic dances, and there were competitions held between the best performers. The winner was often called the dancing philosopher.

We see the use of sacred hand gestures for blessing, divine protection, knowledge, and receiving guidance from the divine in portrayals of Moses. Jesus is also portrayed using stylized hand poses, but most people were not taught the meaning of these gestures, so the people in the Western cultures used them more as expressive communication as they had lost the awareness of their sanctity and healing powers.

From being portrayed in Italian paintings, to use by American Indians, Africans, and Chinese, hand gestures have been used as a form of communication world-wide. Their use is an art that is divinely inspired.

Today, we use hand gestures as a form of communication without much thought. Think about shaking your pointer finger from side to side as a way of saying no or clapping with excitement at the end of a performance to express your gratitude. We greet with a handshake and hold up our hand motionless to stop someone in their tracks. When our palms are turned upward, we are open to receiving guidance. Palms down means we are integrating the wisdom we have received.

Mudras are extremely powerful in that they channel our energy in a specific way leading to a desired outcome.

Mantra

Mantras are ancient Sanskrit healing words used during meditation or mudra practice that when chanted repeatedly have a powerful effect on your being. There are fifty-eight energy points in the hard palate in your mouth which connect to your entire body. When these points are stimulated with sound vibration, it affects your mental and physical energy as certain sounds have healing qualities. When you repeat aloud or whisper these ancient mantras, the meridians on the hard palate are activated in a way that re-patterns the energy of your whole system.

Positive Affirmations

When you meditate, your mind becomes more in tune with your body's needs and your ability to heal is increased. Setting a positive affirmation before your practice will help to guide your focus and energy. Affirmations are always written in the present tense, "I am peaceful," rather than "I will be peaceful." Your mind is in a calm and focused state when you are in a meditation or mudra practice and therefore adding an affirmation to your practice will make it more powerful.

Asana

Asana, meaning comfortable seat in Sanskrit, are the physical postures of yoga. Putting the body into different positions affects the energy of our being.

Six organizing principles to consider while practicing asana are:

1- Notice your body
2- Relax into the body using your breath
3- Set an intention
4- Release perfection
5- Receive energy from the earth
6- Go within and allow the body to express the posture from the inside out

Gratitude

Giving thanks for all the good you have in your life is practicing gratitude. While we all have things we can complain about, we also have plenty grateful for. Focusing on what we appreciate will allow us to see more of the goodness we are surrounded by and also open us up to receive more of it.

Part II

Chapter 4

The Four Pillars of Mindful Motherhood

Pillar 1- Sacred Being

Sacred Being refers to how we interact with ourselves and the situations that come up in our lives. The anecdotes and practices in this section aim to remind you of the beauty of life and being alive, by connecting you to yourself. You will learn how to clear your mind from unnecessary clutter, how to remove the obstacles that keep you from seeing challenging situations clearly, and how to be present to all of life's ups and downs.

I suggest making time in your daily schedule to be with yourself. The time you set aside for this vital self-care, will come to be sacred, and you won't want to go a day without it.

Practicing Presence

When we are present, we are in alignment or in flow. Life is always in motion and ever-changing. If we can recognize this, we can remove the expectation that we are to be "perfect," and connect with the fluidity and cyclical nature of being.

Some moments, days, and seasons of our lives are more challenging than others and being aware of the impermanence of all things can help us get through the tougher times.

My paternal grandmother always used to say to me, "This too shall pass." When I was younger, I didn't fully receive the message. Now that I have more laps around the sun under my belt, I get it. The hard moments won't last forever, and even our most joyous moments are fleeting.

Ride the waves of existence and know that nothing stays the same.

Being Mindful

I had a professor in graduate school who liked to

remind the students in his spirituality and social work class that we are human beings, not human doings. What does it mean to be? How can we be more mindful in our being?

Thich Nhat Hanh speaks of the lamp of mindfulness. He asserts that we each have a lamp of mindfulness that we can light at any time. He says the oil of the lamp is our breathing, our steps, and our peaceful smile. We each need to light our lamp so that our darkness will dissipate and cease. It benefits us to work on lighting our lamps and shining our light.

What is the darkness he speaks of? Are you present to your life or are you just going through the motions?

Create a Positive Affirmation

I invite you to create your own positive affirmation now. Keep in mind it should be written in the present tense as if it is already happening. Make it simple enough that you can memorize it. Tape it to your mirror and your steering wheel. Breathe it in and allow it to become a part of you. You will notice a shift in your life and your being.

A few examples for you to consider as you formulate your own positive affirmation:

I am present in my life. I complete my daily tasks with ease. I joyfully dance with life.

Expressing Gratitude

It is said that what we focus on grows. Have you ever had a day where it seemed that everything that could go wrong, did? You woke up on the wrong side of the bed, were unkind to your children, and broke something. Have you ever had a day where everything flowed beautifully? You awoke filled with joy, had a fun day with your children, and got a prime parking spot.

In both of these situations, you have a choice as to how you respond to them. Even when you are having an off day, there are still good things you can find, and it helps to change your mood if you can acknowledge them. The more you are focusing on something, the more it will manifest. One key to have more amazing days is to practice gratitude.

A simple way to incorporate a gratitude practice into your life is to be thankful for all of the small things. When you rise in the morning, give thanks for a new day. Savor your breakfast and give thanks to all who made it possible, the farmer, the truck driver, the cashier, and so on. Say thank you to the sun for warming you, to your home for shelter, to your vehicle for getting you where you need to be. Express gratitude as much as possible and see if the good increases in your life.

Give Thanks

Martin Seligman created this *Three Good Things* exercise which is designed to be done at night. Here is how to practice:

1- Think of three good things that happened over the course of your day. These can be anything that was positive, the way the sun felt on your face today or even your child saying his or her first word.
2- Write down these three positive things.
3- Reflect on why they happened. Maybe you went for an early morning walk, and the sun greeted you beautifully. Come up with reasons for each event that make sense for you.

Take note of any change in your mood.

Know Thyself

You know your favorite foods, activities, and color, and they are easy for you to recognize and share. But what about your deepest fears?

Fear has a way of distorting our truth, skewing our reality, and dimming our light. When we can understand, befriend, and release our fears, we give ourselves the gift of clear insight and inner peace.

Grab some paper and a pen and set aside a few minutes to complete this fear-releasing exercise.

1- List what angers you—behaviors, thoughts, practices, etc.

2- Can you go deeper and discover why they anger you?

3- What about going even deeper, sending love to them and setting them free?

In which areas of your being do you fear you aren't "good enough?"

Where did those thoughts come from?

Are you able to accept them as part of you? How?

Release them

Let them go.

Tear up the paper and dance in the confetti.

Nurturing Yourself

As moms, we care for others all day long. Whether we are changing diapers, preparing meals, driving to activities, kissing booboos, or tucking children into bed at night, we are constantly doing for and giving to others. It can be easy to lose ourselves in the busyness of it all, or we can see it all as a pathway back home to ourselves. It is our right and responsibility to care for ourselves. Take time for yourself, so you aren't always seeking it, and before it becomes an angry demand.

It has become cliché, but the truth is we cannot give from an empty cup, and we are the only ones that can fill our cups. How we treat ourselves sets the bar for how others will treat us. It is important we create time and space for ourselves daily. When we value ourselves, our children value us.

I invite you now to consider how you will spend your alone time. Where and when will you take it and what you will do.

It doesn't need to look the same every day, but it is important to make it a daily practice. If you only have 3 minutes, take them for yourself. If you miss a day, no problem, just recommit the following day.

Moments of silence and stillness are not empty moments, rather moments of fullness where we experience the presence of our being.

Pay Attention to How Your Inner Voice Speaks to You

Dr. Masaru Emoto discovered that water reacts to thoughts and words that are directed towards it. Water exposed to loving words formed beautiful, colorful, and complex snowflake patterns. In contrast, water exposed to negative thoughts formed incomplete, asymmetrical patterns with dull colors.

Since we are made up of mostly water, the way we talk to ourselves matters.

When you notice yourself experiencing negative self-talk, take a deep breath to quiet that voice and see if you can change those thoughts to more positive ones.

Practicing Self-Study - Svadhyaya

Who am I? What am I? What is my relationship to the world? These are the traditional questions one may ask oneself when doing self-inquiry and I encourage you to relate them to motherhood.

I believe that every mother is majestic, a beautiful part of the universe and nature. While we may all mother differently, the experience of motherhood connects us in profound ways.

Do you have an ideal image of what a mother is supposed to be? Do you compare yourself to TV moms and set unrealistic expectations for yourself?

Take a deep breath and connect with yourself as a mother. What does owning this beautiful title mean to you? How can you appreciate all that you are and all that you will ever be as a mother?

Internalize

Positive Affirmations for Mothering

I am the best mother for my child/ren.
I am loving and kind and share love easily with my child/ren.

Say them, believe them, internalize them.

Honoring Intuition's Voice

Sometimes, as mothers, we will be in a situation where we feel we do not have the answer, but the truth is we always have it within. If we are able to recognize, know, and follow our intuition, we find ourselves able to act on a decision more easily.

Yes, there will be times when we make the "wrong" decision, or there is more than one right option. We are human and knowing how to navigate any choice we make is innate to our being, so we can relax a bit knowing we will never go too far astray. Life is a journey we are living and creating daily, not a final destination.

Connect with Your Intuition

To connect with your intuition, practice by asking yourself a simple question and then being in stillness for a moment to receive the answer. Drop into your body and notice where you feel the answer. After you've done this, start asking more complex questions, return to stillness, come out of your mind and take note where you feel the answer in your body. The more you practice "hearing" your intuition, the easier it will become.

In the times where you are still unsure, give way to love. Love is always the best answer.

Spending Time Wisely

Time passes whether we are conscious of it or not. Some days seem to drag on forever, while others pass in the blink of an eye. To get the most out of each day, aim to have time together, alone time, work time, and play time.

I often tell people I am a slow mom in an "insta" world. Surrounded by Instant Pot to cook your food quickly, Instacart to deliver your groceries at the push of a button, Instagram as the abbreviated version of Facebook, and insta-everything it seems, it takes our effort to be sure we are creating the time and space for the things we desire.

How do you desire to spend your time?

Enable Self-Discovery

Motherhood helps us find ourselves; it is both a practice and a spiritual journey that awakens our highest self if we allow it. Every small action we take mindfully is a part of self-discovery.

Daily mindfulness leads to the awareness of when to sacrifice or nurture ourselves. The more in tune we are with our being, the easier it is to honor what we need. Being aware of all the ways we can care for ourselves, allows us to share the same care with our children.

Children are mirrors that reflect what is inside of us. Their growth is an opportunity to heal our pain, go deeper within and become more human.

My saddest tears and my loudest laughs have been experienced since I became a mom. I recognize the world as a brighter place, and, at times, life can also feel scarier. Finding space for internalizing and expressing my emotions is a daily practice.

The more we know about ourselves, the more we discover about our children. Once something is part of our reality, it can't cease to exist. When you've experienced pure joy, you will seek it more. When you discover a new food that you love, you will never forget it. Taste all the flavors and explore the depth of your being.

Choosing Love over Fear

Fear and love cannot exist in the same second. I have the quote, "Don't let fear kill the magic" on my vision board to serve as a reminder of the magic of motherhood. Often, when we are triggered by our children's behavior, it's because it hits a deep insecurity or fear within us.

When our children do something that worries us or doesn't meet a standard we have set in our mind, the fear sets in and the doubts start emerging.

> "What if they aren't good enough at math or reading?"
> "Why is she doing it that way?"
> "Will other children accept him if he chooses to dress that way?"

All of the doubts that run through our heads can take over and keep us in a state of worry if we don't keep them in check.

When we are able to identify our wounds and fears, we can then understand, accept, and release them.

Release Fear

Take a moment to identify one fear you have about your children.

Think about it for a minute and try to discover where it is coming from.

Once you know, send love to the thought, and to yourself.

Let it go! Our power lies within us, always.

Love heals.

Holding Space

Our shadow side emotions—anger, fear, guilt, jealousy, and resentment—will consume us if we allow them to. When we hold on to these feelings instead of allowing them to be expressed, they build up inside of us and we eventually "lose it". If we are able to express them as they come up, we can then work through them, instead of them taking over our entire being.

Emptying the cup before it overflows gives us the opportunity to release the emotions safely. When we can safely release our emotions, we are afforded the opportunity to model a healthy outlet for our children, and we can offer grace and hold space for their big emotions as they appear.

Everything we feel and experience is safe for us to express. The challenge is releasing any judgments we may hold about these tougher to express emotions, and finding ways to allow them to be, without fully consuming us.

Spiritual Evolution

I am part of a business mastermind group, and we meet Sunday mornings to support and encourage each other. One week, we were discussing our frustrations with how long it was taking to make money in our businesses, which led to talking about spiritual development and personal growth.

We all shared similar thoughts, feelings, and frustrations.

"The same lessons keep showing up for me, over and over."

"Is there even an end to this path?"

"Some days I feel as if I haven't done any of the work at all."

"I just want to be enlightened already."

While we were speaking, it became clear to me that we are always changing and evolving, always works in progress. Every day is a new beginning. Of course, since I am always thinking about motherhood,

I immediately internalized the lesson and thought about how it applied to being a mom.

Each moment we show up and strive to do our best. Some days it means we engage with our children with ease, and others it means every part of the day is a struggle. This is the practice of motherhood. Recognizing the natural rhythm of our emotions is part of the enlightenment we all seek. Accepting our humanity and remaining present in our lives.

Words Carry Weight

Somewhere along this path of motherhood, I encountered words that have been life-altering, they are: "I get to." There are always a million and one things to be doing as a mom, and I was finding myself always saying, "I have to . . ." What a heavy way to express something that needs to be completed.

"I have to make breakfast, wash the dishes, clean up the kitchen, and pack snacks for the day." It's heavy and draining of energy. I feel tired just reading it! But with the simple shifting of words from "I have to" to "I get to," we can change the way we process and internalize the work we need to do. The energy is lighter, and it doesn't feel as draining.

The same tasks can be completed without

burdening ourselves with the weight of the words. "I get to make breakfast, wash the dishes, clean up the kitchen, and pack snacks for the day."

While it may seem unnatural at first, with time, you will begin to notice how the simple change of a word shifts your reality ever so slightly.

Conscious Consumption

Everything we consume becomes a part of our being—food, drinks, media, advertising, books, video games, all of it. As an introverted empath, some days social media is too overwhelming for me. My feed is mostly filled with high-vibe, consciousness-raising information, but since we can't control what other people post and what Facebook decides to show us, sometimes I am exposed to images and information I would rather not consume.

We are constantly bombarded with information, billboards, ads on the radio, subliminal messages in commercials, images in magazines, and of course, the words we hear from others. What are you consuming? Does it fill you up or deplete you?

Take Notes

Take an inventory of everything you consume in a

typical hour, and consider removing the sources that don't benefit your being.

Express Emotions

If we pay attention, children can be the greatest teachers. They live in the present and their imaginations; they allow their emotions to flow with ease and without attachment. When they cry, they let it all out. Their laughter consumes their entire being. They welcome and express their emotions, and then move on.

When my children fight, they fully express what is on their minds. Sometimes they kick and scream and it gets so wild, and when they have gotten all their anger out, they move on as if they never fought. Once they feel their point has been made, and their voice heard, they return to play. Forgiveness comes easily to them.

Emotional Freedom

Practice expressing your emotions the way children do. Let it all out, and then move on. Release the desire to live a single incident numerous times as withholding emotions and feelings will cause them to reappear at some other time, causing harm or havoc for yourself and others.

Sacred Pauses

In the busyness of motherhood, we can forget to pause. During your day, incorporate short, sacred pauses where you have nothing else to do but focus on being present.

I often find that it is easy for me to create this space while in the car. I am already seated and focused on driving, and adding some conscious, deep breaths to it, is no biggie.

Taking these mini-breaks allows me to be the "after you" driver and not the one speeding in front of you to cut you off.

Another place where you can incorporate a sacred pause is in the shower. Breathe in all the goodness available to you and allow anything weighing you down to slide down the drain with the water that cleansed your body.

The Power of "Be-ing"

Simply "be" and release the need to "do" a few times a day and you will see how small changes can have significant impact.

Peace Spreads

As human beings, we are affected by the energy

of those in our proximity. One peaceful person in the family can share that peace with others, just as one toxic person in the family can spread toxicity.

Since recovering from the vertigo attack, I've made it a priority to wake up before my family to have time for self-care, and part of my morning routine is meditating. On the mornings I decide to skip it because I feel I have too much work to do, there is a noticeable difference in the flow of the day.

The energy is more frenetic. The children seem grumpier, and I am certainly quicker to get frustrated.

When the children wake up and join me in meditation, it's truly a sight to be seen. They are more peaceful. The morning hugs are sweeter. There aren't too many complaints when they are told what's for breakfast, and what the plans for the day are.

Our vibe affects our tribe and finding the silence within the noise helps us to find peace. We can always remove ourselves from a crazy situation, turn inward, and share our calm with others.

Clear Your Mind

The running to-do lists we carry in our minds serve a purpose but often take us away from the space where we can just be. A dear friend taught me a beautiful practice, brain dumping, and I am happy to share it with you as it can be life-changing.

Brain Dump

In order to "brain dump" you will need the following: paper, a writing utensil, and as much time as it takes you to clear the to-do list from your mind. 50 minutes is the suggested time, but I am usually able to complete mine in about 30 minutes.

Sit in a comfortable place where you won't be disturbed for the duration of the practice.

Quiet your mind and begin to jot down all the little thoughts floating around. Get them all out! Changing light bulbs, a phone call you need to make, a question you have for a friend, items you need to purchase, and anything else that comes up.

Notice how much more space you now have for being?

Pillar 2- Open-Hearted Relationships

"You can sit and meditate while your baby cries herself to sleep. Or you can go to her and share her tears, and find yourself." - Vimala McClure

In open-hearted relationships, there is space for all parties involved to be and express who they are freely. You can show all sides of yourself and accept the same of your children. There are practices included in this section of the book which will aid you in deepening the bond you have with your children, showing them that they matter and you see them for who they are, and also a few gentle reminders to be flexible when the situation permits.

Incorporating some of these practices into your mothering can be as easy as hugging your child, and the results you experience can be relationship changing.

Unity is Strength

We were gifted a beautiful wall hanging with an Adinkra symbol meaning "unity is strength" for our wedding. Every time I pass by it, it serves as a beautiful reminder to stay connected with my family members.

The truth is, relationships take work, all of them. Of course, we love our children, and they also know how to push our buttons in a way no one else can. They see us as our whole selves and love us with their entire being.

Staying united makes the relationship stronger. Working through all the daily ups and downs, the small disagreements, and the big ones, fortifies the relationship and creates more unity. I tell my children all the time that we can accomplish anything we set out to, together.

As mothers we are the center of the family like the Sun is to the planets in our solar system. Our presence and energy affect the entire family, and when we can take time to fill our cup, our light can shine brighter. How we mother matters, and I express this not to add anything else to your already full plate, but to let you know how treasured you are.

When we take the time to strengthen the foundation of love with our children and make sure it is solid, the times where we encounter upsets will not shake the foundation. They may add some booboos, but nothing damaging enough to destroy it. Our children accept our humanity and our perfect imperfection. Following their lead and allowing ourselves grace is the best way to stay present and deepen the bond with them.

It is said that there is an 80/20 rule when it comes to mothering. If we are our best selves 80 percent of the time, that is what our children will remember. This allows for our perfect imperfection, and the "mommy monster" to show 20 percent of the time without affecting the relationship. We are all works in progress, and forgiveness comes easily to our children. With each breath, we can start over.

Strengthen the Foundation of Love with Your Child/ren

Connect with your child/ren through daily chores. Involve them in your tasks like laundry, dishes, and setting the table. Mine love to spray the glass and wipe it clean. They feel good helping you, and it also serves as a way to connect. Some of the most intimate stories are shared with me while getting clean clothes out of the dryer to be folded.

See your children for who they are. Our children show us how they prefer to be mothered. All the answers we seek, are within our relationship with our child, and there is no need to look outside the relationship for the answers. Look within yourself and your child.

Create a morning routine that gets the day off to a good start. How we begin the day sets the tone for the entire day.

What is the first thing you do in the morning? Check your phone? Make coffee? Exercise?

Does it feel nourishing to you? If not, try to see how you can make it so.

In my family, this means I wake up first to write, exercise, and meditate. I know I need some quiet time in the morning to be alone in order to prepare for the day ahead, and to be sure I'm starting my day with a clear head and not doing for others before I've taken care of myself. When my children wake up, I feel nourished and full, ready to begin the day with them.

Give hugs. Touch brings us to the present moment and calms our mind and body. Hugging is a great way to connect and greet your child/ren when they wake up in the morning or after you've been apart. Try to hold the hug for at least four breaths and allow your child to be the one to end the hug. Extra points if they allow you to kiss them too. (Sometimes some of my children prefer no kiss, and I honor their choice.)

Remember to play. Have fun and be silly. Fully immerse yourself in whatever you are playing. When we play, we are automatically transported to the present moment and filled with feel-good chemicals. Our minds relax, and we can just be.

Make eye contact. When speaking with your child/ren, squat down to their level and look them in the eyes. Send love through your eyes, and you will both experience increased well-being and physical health because of the emotional connection you share.

Spend quality time with each child as often as possible. Try taking a few minutes daily to connect with your child/ren. Even five minutes alone with you where they get to choose the activity or topic of conversation is enough to strengthen your bond and for the child to know you are a safe place for them to communicate their feelings.

Make your dinner table a sacred place. Shared meals nourish our bodies and spirits. I understand life is busy and it isn't always possible to eat meals together, but whenever possible, sit at the table and share mealtime with your family.

The rule in our home is no electronics at the table. This is so we can all come together and be present to enjoy each other's company. I always try to ask how everyone's day went, what they liked best, and what was most challenging for them.

Think of your kitchen table as the anchor of the

family. It holds you all together. It is the place for connecting and being.

On Friday nights, I light candles for dinner, and we review how the week went. Each child receives a blessing, and also gets to share their favorite part of the week and what was most challenging for them that week. Saturdays are a no/low technology day.

Often, the children say the best part of their week is "right now," while we are all together sharing our special meal of the week. These are the moments that they treasure, the times of togetherness.

Have a peaceful bedtime routine. By the end of the day, I am beat, and sometimes when my children get out their last bits of energy, it pushes me over the edge. I have very little left to give and sometimes bedtime doesn't go as smoothly as I'd like.

If you know you are spent by bedtime, try to take 2 minutes to "gear up" and center before you begin the bedtime routine. In my home, I remind my crew that after dinner, it is calming down time. Time to start winding down from the day and preparing to go to bed. Sometimes we play games, we meditate together, or I read to my children, and then they brush their teeth and get their final hug and kiss of the day before bed.

Getting children to sleep. My youngest still nurses

to sleep and my older three have varied requests to help them transition to dreamland. My oldest likes to tell stories to his two younger brothers. My second son likes when I do the "screens," and my youngest son likes me to rub his back. They all want that last bit of connection before sleeping.

The screens exercise script

Close your eyes and imagine there are screens on the backs of your eyelids. Choose something that makes you feel relaxed and picture it there. Maybe it's an ocean wave, the stars in the sky, a butterfly flying through the air, or a feather floating by. Take deep breaths as you watch whatever calms you. Keep taking deep breaths and watching your movie until you feel very relaxed and ready to sleep.

Being present. The greatest gift we can give our children is our true presence. Listening when they speak, playing with them, and making sure we have time where they are the only thing we are focusing on. This means we need to put our phones down and pay complete attention to them throughout the day. Our children feel so special and loved when receiving special attention from us; their smiles say it all.

Focus on the Who Not the What

I've caught myself a few times saying things like, "My son is good at math, but not as quick with the reading," or "He is the less athletic of the two." When we evaluate our children, or ourselves, based on our achievements, we are valuing the outcome more than the process.

Labels can be hurtful. I remember when I was assigned to the "fast readers" group in 5th grade, and I can still recall the looks of embarrassment on the faces of the children who were placed in the "slow readers" group. We have a way of living up or down to people's expectations of us.

When I find myself categorizing my children, I remind myself of the beauty of diversity. Not everyone on the planet is an astrophysicist and thank goodness for that. We are all unique and beautiful in our own special ways.

Focus on the unique value each child brings, and not his or her shortcomings. Value the process. We are all being and becoming who we are meant to be.

Showing Children They Matter

We all want to be seen, heard, understood, and

appreciated. Listening to your children when they speak is a wonderful way to show them they matter to you.

Our children desire to know they are special, important, and loved. When possible, get down to eye level when speaking with your child and look them in the eyes. Let them know you see them and treasure them.

I've talked to nearly 30,000 people on this show, and all 30,000 had one thing in common: They all wanted validation. If I could reach through this television and sit on your sofa or sit on a stool in your kitchen right now, I would tell you that every single person you will ever meet shares that common desire. They want to know: 'Do you see me? Do you hear me? Does what I say mean anything to you? Understanding that one principle, that everybody wants to be heard, has allowed me to hold the microphone for you all these years with the least amount of judgment. Now I can't say I wasn't judging some days. Some days, I had to judge just a little bit. But it's helped me to stand and to try to do that with an open mind and to do it with an open heart. It has worked for this platform, and I guarantee you it will work for yours. Try it with your children, your husband, your wife, your boss, your friends. Validate them. 'I see you. I hear you. And what you say matters to me.'

~Oprah Winfrey, May 25, 2011

"Shoulds" and "Nots" the Four-Letter Words of Motherhood

I should be this way, not the way I am. I should have known better. I should do . . .

Not over there! Not that way!

Who likes being told what to do all the time? My guess is that most of us prefer some freedom and flexibility in our day, and our children have that same desire. Focusing on "shoulds" and "nots" breeds resistant energy.

When we feel like we are under a microscope and on a tight leash, we want to rebel. Currently, my 2-year-old is not fond of getting her diaper changed. She is potty learning, and sometimes she wants to wear underwear, and other times she prefers a diaper. She has to be the one to choose, not me.

"She should be using the potty by now; all of her brothers were. This is not the way to potty train; why doesn't she just do what I want?" are some of the thoughts I notice running through my mind. No wonder she is so feisty about it. I'm "shoulding" all over her!

When we allow for flexibility, it creates more ease in our mothering.

Use of Power

There are always many ways to handle a challenging situation with our children. As mothers, we possess a special power, just by being who we are. Our word is often the final word, and it is ideal if we are able to resolve the issue without over-exerting our authority. Using your "I mean it voice" instead of yelling, shows power combined with calm.

"Because I said so and I'm the mom." The magical words that can change the direction of a conversation and allow us to "win" any disagreement with our children. This use of power gives us the result we are seeking but doesn't get to the heart of the issue.

While the use of power works, it may not always be the most desirable way to get what we want. If we overuse it, it will decrease in effectiveness, and our children may come to resent or fear us. Think about the story of the boy who cried wolf. When there really was a situation, no one believed him because he had been playing around with his use of power.

Before relying on power, consider:
1- Is there another way to accomplish the goal?
2- What are my choices?
3- How can I get a desirable result without yelling?

Bend, Don't Break

"Will this matter in 5 years?" is a question I have been asking myself a lot lately. Sometimes, we don't know the answer or our children's behavior doesn't go according to our plans, and that's ok. Allowing some wiggle room and focusing on the big picture is far easier than trying to control every small detail.

A challenge that's been happening in my home is when my children want to eat a little snack before bed, after their teeth are brushed. At first, I would tell them they could not eat after brushing their teeth, but now I am not as rigid about it. Holding onto the "no food after brushing teeth rule" so intensely caused a lot of upset in my home, and after a few days and some tears shed, I realized I would rather have them brush again than go to sleep hungry.

While structure and routine are important for maintaining the flow in my home, there are only a few rules that can't be bent.

When doubt arises, give way to love. Come back to center and know love is more important. Allow love to be your compass.

Ways to Make Up

Sometimes we lose our patience; we are human and can only take so much. Our children forgive us for our perfect imperfection, and it serves us best to allow ourselves that same grace.

I've found that once I've calmed down after a "freak out," when I've yelled at my children, apologizing, and meaning it, is what seems to heal the situation the fastest. An effective apology framework to follow is explaining what triggered you, why you reacted the way you did, and how you will try to respond better in the future. Ask the child why they did what they did and if there is a way they can do things differently in the future.

Another way we settle disagreements in our home is to call a family meeting. During the meeting, we sit in a circle, and everyone has a chance to express themselves. When one person is speaking, the others are quiet to let the speaker know their thoughts are valued, and it is safe to express them.

And lastly, hugs are healing. Once the situation has calmed, ask all parties involved (including yourself) if a hug would feel good at that time. After we've been upset and our energy was crazy, it always feels good to come back to center with a hug.

Pillar 3- Magical Movements

Positioning our bodies in certain ways aids us in shifting our energy to change how we are feeling. The wisdom held in these movements is ancient, and when we can fully tune into what we are doing, we will notice a change in our emotional state. Many of the practices can be completed anywhere and at any time, even when you are playing with your children at the playground.

Be gentle with your body. If something feels painful or uncomfortable, don't do it. You can always reach out to me, and I will provide you with an alternate posture or a gentler variation.

The Value of Our Breath

Our breath is vital to our existence. Oftentimes we inhale and exhale without giving any thought to it. Today, I invite you to spend some time consciously breathing—being present with each inhale and each exhale. Breathing in to nourish your being and exhaling to cleanse your being. Our breath is an ever-present friend that never fails to calm and center us, bringing us back to the present moment, as life unfolds.

Take a Deep Breath

Allow yourself some time alone to do this exercise. Begin by taking notice of your natural breath. Just breathe and be. There is nothing to be done right now but to focus on your breath. Begin to breathe only through your nose; inhaling and exhaling through the nostrils. Maybe you would like to count the length of each breath. Inhaling for a count of four and exhaling to a four count. Think of something you would like to release from your life and something you would like to enhance. Maybe you want to release anger or fear, and maybe you'd like to enhance patience or peace. Enhance on the inhale, release on the exhale. Sit or lie in a comfortable position and place one hand on your abdomen and one on your chest. As you inhale, the bottom hand moves first then the top. As you exhale, your top hand moves then your bottom. Start lengthening and deepening each breath. Be present with the breath and feel how each inhale fills you up with goodness and each exhale releases negativity. Continue to do this for as long as you like, at least a full three minutes.

Do you feel different after focusing on your breath? Are there ways you can use this practice throughout your day while you are mothering?

Releasing Anger

Oftentimes when we get angry or frustrated, we can feel emotion building in our physical body. We all have a breaking point, the place where the level of negative energy becomes too much, and we lose it—whatever that may mean for you. When we are aware of the anger building in our body, we can take the necessary actions to release it. Feel what is beneath the anger—fear, doubt, self-protection. Once acknowledge the cause, we can accept and release it.

One day I was at the pool with my children and my aunt. My oldest started to mock everything I said, and I could feel my frustration level rising. He kept doing it and then my second son joined in. I could feel the anger bubbling in my body. Lucky for me, my wonderful aunt was with us and could see I was getting frustrated, so she decided to turn it into a game. She pointed at her head and said, "M T," and my sons followed suit. I started laughing hysterically, and my sons didn't know why, which made it that much funnier. After a few minutes of them pointing at their heads and saying "empty," I filled them in on the joke, and they also began to laugh.

When we are able to let things go, it often feels much better than holding the negativity inside. A release of anger was just what I had needed!

Another way to move energy and release it is by moving the body. A handy asana, yoga posture, to know is mountain pose. Mountain may seem like a simple pose but it is far from that and practicing it can greatly aid you in reshaping your mental state, energy flow, and your physical body.

Release Anger
Mountain Pose-Tadasana

Ground through your feet. Spread all ten toes and find equal weight in the four corners of your feet: the ball mound of the big toe, the ball mound of the little toe, the outer heel, and the inner heel.

Firm your quadriceps and slightly rotate the inner thighs backward.

To engage your core, lengthen your tailbone and draw your pubic bone up, as your draw your hip points in toward your navel.

Breathe into your back body and lift your sternum.

Root your shoulder blades against your back ribs.

Lift through the crown of your head and soften your gaze.

Imagine roots growing from your feet to deep into the Earth and sucking up whatever energy you need while you continue to release anger and breathe deeply.

Release from the posture when you feel ready.

Keeping up with Children

As a mother, you know children demand attention, guidance, wisdom, patience, and presence. They crave acknowledgment and reassurance from you. Sometimes they ask for so much that you have nothing left to give! Our days are filled with giving to our children, sometimes only having enough time for ourselves to use the bathroom. Or maybe you don't even get that. I think most moms can relate to little eyes staring at them while they are on the toilet.

You desire a break, a way to recharge your battery. While an actual getaway may not be possible, you can always take a few minutes to practice this mudra for keeping up with children without depleting your energy and calm.

Renew Energy

Sit in a comfortable position with your legs crossed. Lengthen your spine.

Make circles with the tips of your thumbs and index fingers. The other fingers are relaxed but extended outward. Rest the hands palms facing upward, on the knees. Use your long, deep breathing to calm and relax you.

Mantra: You can repeat the mantra mentally:

> AAD SUCH
> JUGAAD SUCH
> HAI BHEE SUCH
> NANAK HOSEE
> BHEE SUCH

(True in the beginning, true in all ages, true at present, true it shall ever be.)

Breath: Long, deep, and slow

Continue for three minutes and feel relaxed and renewed.

Surrender to Challenging Situations

How do you deal with unpleasant situations? Do you spend time agonizing about them or are you able to surrender to the situation, not spending more energy on it than necessary?

One day, upon returning to my car after grocery shopping at Whole Foods and buckling my four children in, I started the car only to realize the steering wheel wouldn't turn. It was drizzling, lightning, and you could hear thunder in the distance. A big storm was on its way. Lucky for me, my aunt was there, and she called AAA. They told her they would be there within an hour's time. OK, that wasn't so bad I thought to myself. I would just wait in the car with my children until AAA arrived. I called my husband to tell him about the steering wheel, and he said he would make his way to us. The storm was getting worse. You get the idea; it was one of those situations where I could have freaked out and gotten angry or upset, but instead, I consciously decided to surrender and allow the situation to unfold naturally. It all ended up working out in the end, as situations like that always seem to do.

Become aware of your automatic response when confronting difficulty and see if you can surrender to life's duality. Without the bad, we cannot have the good. Everything in existence has two sides to it. This is the natural way of the universe. When we allow ourselves to accept this reality, we suffer less, and we appreciate the good even more.

Let Go

Child's Pose - Balasana

Kneel down and let the tops of your feet rest on the floor. Touch your big toes together. Then lower your hips back and sit on your heels.

Join your knees together or separate them hip-distance apart.

Hinge at the hips and slowly fold forward. Rest the torso over your thighs if the knees are joined, and between your thighs, if the knees are wide.

Extend your arms in front of you and place the palms down on the mat. Or extend the arms behind you, alongside your torso, with palms facing up.

Release your shoulders toward the ground and rest your forehead (third eye) on the mat in front of your knees.

Keep your hands and arms engaged in Child's pose. Reach forward or backward depending on your hand placement.

Stay here for a few minutes. Trust the natural rhythm and flow of life.

Cultivating Balance

As part of my yoga teacher's training, I studied Hatha Yoga. "Ha" meaning sun, in Sanskrit, and "Tha" meaning moon. When practicing hatha yoga, movement is always coordinated with the breath, and every posture is counterbalanced with another posture. If you do a backbend, you will also always do a forward fold. If you do a movement on the right side of the body, you will do the same movement on the left side of the body.

Nothing is in existence without its counterpart.

One morning during breakfast my six-year-old was naming opposites. He covered day and night, sun and moon, roots and branches, left and right, hot and cold, dark and light, positive and negative, mountain and valley. It was so beautiful to witness his recognition of the workings of the universe.

Within our being, opposites are in existence, and I believe when we can recognize and honor this fact, it allows us to express our humanity more fully. We possess both male and female energies. We experience happiness and sadness, peace and chaos, craziness and balance. It is all a part of our human reality.

Root and Grow
Tree Pose - Vriksasana

This is one of my favorite balancing postures. We root our feet in the ground while extending the spine long and "growing" the crown of the head. It creates inner peace and balance.

Start in Mountain Pose. Find a gazing point; this is vital for balancing postures!

Bend the right knee and bring the sole of the right foot to your ankle, your calf, or your inner thigh. Ground through the four corners of your left foot.

Find a place for your arms. I like mine to be palms touching at heart center. Perhaps you would like yours in a "T" or extended upward like branches.

Once you have found your tree pose, stay here until you are ready to gently release. No worries if you fall out of it, just laugh and try again. It's part of the fun!

Repeat on the other side.

Calling on Patience

Our children are our greatest teachers. Being with them is like constantly looking in a mirror. They reflect our strengths and the areas that would serve us to work on by the behaviors they express.

Conscious mothering takes a lot of patience. Children fight. They ask the same question 10,000 times. They run when they aren't supposed to. They take forever to put on their shoes. And they know just how to push our buttons and alert us to an opportunity for personal growth. I believe mothering is easier when we can cultivate patience and come up with ways to curb our frustrations. It takes our conscious effort to not go from kind mother to mommy monster at the smallest provocation.

What can you do to cultivate patience on days when your fuse is short?

How can you repair your relationship with your child after you have "lost it"?

Patience is a virtue that everyone can develop. This mudra will help you transform your frustration and aid you in becoming more patient and tolerant.

Release Frustration

Sit in a comfortable seated position with a straight back. Make circles with the tips of your thumbs and middle fingers, keeping the other fingers straight. Upper arms are parallel to the floor, arms out like goal posts. Your hands are at ear level, palms facing front, and fingers pointing toward the sky.

Mantra: EK ONG KAR SAT GURU PRASAAD

(One creator, illuminated by G-d's Grace)

Breathe deeply and observe yourself becoming calmer and more patient with each breath.

Harnessing Truthfulness

As a mother, what does it mean to be honest with yourself and others? To live with integrity and honesty?

It was one of those days. Everything was crazy at home. The children were fighting non-stop, and I could feel my anger building. I was ready to scream my head off. I knew that approach never worked; it only made the energy around us more chaotic. So, what did I do instead? I calmly told my children to sit down where they were, and I told them the truth.

I shared with them how their fighting was making me feel. I didn't scream. I didn't yell. I spoke my truth, and it felt amazing.

Being truthful isn't always an easy thing to do. Sometimes it means going against the crowd. It may even be that speaking the truth could hurt somebody's feelings. For mothers, being honest is vital because it keeps us accountable. "Honesty is the best policy," was always the motto in my home growing up, and I am teaching my children the same. By honoring your truth, you give others permission to do the same.

Welcoming Honesty
Lion Pose-Simhasana

Kneel on the floor. Lift your sitting bones and cross your legs at the ankles, so your feet face the sides of your mat. Then sit back on the top heel.

Place the left hand on the left knee and right hand on the right knee. Extend your arms, spread your fingers out wide, and press your palms firmly against the knees.

Inhale through your nose and open your mouth wide. Stretch your tongue out and down, toward your chin, as far as you can.

With your tongue sticking out, exhale and let out a powerful, audible breath. The exhalation should mimic a roar, making the "ha" sound.

Set your gaze upward between your eyebrows or to the tip of your nose.

Stay in Lion pose for 30 seconds, roaring up to three times. Then switch the crossing of your legs and repeat on the other side.

This posture will help you to speak your truth.

Increasing Concentration

The phone is ringing. The baby is crying. The water on the stovetop is boiling over, and you have to pee. The scenario may look different in your home, but the idea is the same. As mothers, we are constantly being pulled in so many directions which makes it even more important for us to take time to focus.

An old Cherokee is teaching his grandson about life. "A fight is going on inside me," he said to the boy.

"It is a terrible fight, and it is between two wolves. One is evil – he is anger, envy, sorrow, regret, greed, arrogance, self-pity, guilt, resentment, inferiority, lies, false pride, superiority, and ego." He continued, "The other is good – he is joy, peace, love, hope, serenity, humility, kindness, benevolence, empathy, generosity, truth, compassion, and faith. The same fight is going on inside you – and inside every other person, too."

The grandson thought about it for a minute and then asked his grandfather, "Which wolf will win?"

The old Cherokee simply replied, "The one you feed."

What we focus on grows. We can choose to get caught up in the chaos, or we can choose to breathe, calm ourselves, and take one action at a time. This breathing technique will help to calm you and allow you to focus on being more present and mindful while mothering.

Concentrate on the Now

Nadi Shodana- Alternate Nostril Breathing

Sit comfortably with your spine long and shoulders relaxed. Keep a gentle smile on your face.

Place your left hand on the left knee, palms open to the sky.

Place the tip of the index finger and middle finger of the right hand in between the eyebrows, the ring finger and little finger on the left nostril, and the thumb on the right nostril. We will use the ring finger and little finger to open or close the left nostril and thumb for the right nostril.

Press your thumb down on the right nostril and breathe out gently through the left nostril.

Now breathe in from the left nostril and then

press the left nostril gently with the ring finger and little finger. Removing the right thumb from the right nostril, breathe out from the right.

Breathe in from the right nostril and exhale from the left. You have now completed one round of Nadi Shodhana pranayama. Continue inhaling and exhaling from alternate nostrils.

Complete nine such rounds by alternately breathing through both nostrils. After every exhalation, remember to breathe in from the same nostril from which you exhaled. Keep your eyes closed throughout and continue taking long, deep, smooth breaths without any force or effort.

Recharge Your Being

A tree has roots. A house has a foundation. Where do you gather strength from when it feels you have nothing left to give?

I was having one of those days. The days we'd rather not discuss with the world. My children were in rare form, and I must have woken up on the wrong side of the bed. All I wanted to do was make my children disappear so that I could snuggle in bed with a good book. Since there was no way to make that scenario a reality, I knew I had to dig deep within myself and find a way to ground my energy. For me, that meant taking my children outside for a long walk so they could get their crazies out, and I could gather energy and joy from the earth. Being outside fills my cup and grounds me. It allows me to recharge and reset.

Maybe what grounds you is a hot mug of tea, a hike in the woods, or a dip in the ocean. Do you have an alternative if your traditional grounding methods are not available? Here is one you can add to your repertoire, a recharging mudra.

It is beneficial to know how to recharge and rejuvenate our minds and bodies to keep up with our daily demands. This mudra builds up energy throughout your system and gives you a greater capacity for dealing with life's challenges and tasks. It fills you up with a new vibrant force.

Energize Your Mind

Sit in a comfortable seated position with a long spine and extend your arms straight out in front of you, parallel to the ground. Make a fist with your right hand. Wrap your left fingers around the fist, with the bases of the palms touching, thumbs close together and extended straight up. Focus your eyes on the thumbs.

Breath: Long, deep, and slow

Continue for a few minutes and relax and recharge.

The Beauty of Simplicity

Vimala from *The Tao of Motherhood* writes,

Keep your life simple, and serenity will follow. Like a small country with little need for supersonic travel, a simple life has little need for tension and stress. Give your children yourself, and the need for things is minimal. Mothering requires a lot of action and doing, but there are times when no specific activity demands your attention. They are the quiet moments that may be few and far between, yet they are cherished.

Pay attention to what happens in your mind and body in these moments. Are you able to just be? Or are you searching for something to occupy your attention—music, a phone call, food, or a book? See if you can resist the impulse toward busyness or distraction and simply rest in that moment.

Initially, these moments of stillness may feel uncomfortable, but see if you can allow them to be, so that you can enjoy the simplicity of being. Let these quiet moments be a source of renewal and creativity.

Our children benefit most from our true presence.

Just Be

As you sit in meditation today, focus on your breath and only your breath.

See if you can integrate this presence to the time you spend with your children. Can you put all distractions aside and just be with them? Watch as the magic of togetherness unfolds.

Call on Integrity

According to Merriam-Webster, the definition of integrity is the quality of being honest and fair; the state of being complete or whole.

Even when faced with an extreme challenge, it serves us well always to have integrity. How can we best respond to a challenge instead of reacting to it? Respond, not react. Mindful responding over mindless reacting. In maintaining our integrity, we can save ourselves and our loved ones from a lot of sorrow, regret, and unnecessary pain.

This mudra will strengthen your ability to keep your presence of mind and integrity so that you can make healthier choices and responses under stress.

Respond, Don't React

Sit with a long spine, your arms out in goal posts. Bring your hands to ear level, palms out. Curl your fingers inward so that they touch the palms. Extend your thumbs straight out and point them toward your temples.

Mantra: SAT NAM

(Truth is G-d's name, One in Spirit)

Breath: Long, deep, and slow

Practice for at least three minutes, then relax.

Practice Self-Empathy

Are you able take time to listen to what you need to feel nourished? Practicing self-empathy and being in tune with your own needs and feelings is vital to be an effective mother. Knowing when it's time for an internal reset is a huge part of cultivating inner peace, as it prevents us from reaching our breaking points.

How do you celebrate your "good" days? Are you able to honor yourself when you are burnt-out and take time to recharge? Are you kind to yourself?

Hug yourself! Allow yourself the same grace you extend to others. Forgive yourself and move on. Celebrate your victories no matter how small they seem. Go ahead and do it!

Give yourself a little foot massage and thank yourself for all the hard work you do.

Celebrate You

Foot Massage.

With your shoes off, place a ball on the ground in front of you; you can be seated or standing.

Roll your right foot forward and backward slowly on the ball.

Next, apply pressure until you feel a pull, but not enough to cause pain. Roll your foot side to side.

Place your heel on the ball to make circular motions.

Roll your foot, so the ball massages the arch of your foot.

Repeat with the left foot.

If you don't have a ball . . .

While seated, cross the right foot over the left leg and roll your ankles, stretch your toes, and rub your thumb in a circular motion over the sole of your entire foot. When you feel ready, switch to the left foot.

Bedtime Mudra for a Good Morning

The way we feel in the morning affects our entire day. Practicing this mudra at bedtime will help you de-stress before bed, have a better night's sleep, and wake up positive and rested, ready for the day.

As you practice this mudra, visualize a ball of white light above your head.

Sit with a long spine, elbows extended to the sides, hands a few inches in front of the body, just above the navel. Your palms are facing up. Curl your thumb around the index fingertips and extend the other fingers so that they touch each other back to back. Keep your palms up, left hand on top of the right.

Mantra: HAR HARE WAHE, HAR HARE WAHE
(G-d is the creator of supreme power and wisdom)
Breath: Inhale six short breaths as you mentally repeat the mantra, exhale one strong breath.

Continue for three minutes, building the practice to eleven minutes if you so desire.

Increase Awareness

Have you ever observed ants? They are amazing little creatures. Every time two ants cross paths, they greet each other. This was an amazing observation I made while serving in the Peace Corps, living in the Dominican Republic where life is not as fast-paced as it is in the U.S.

My oldest son had the idea that our family should perform the same ritual, so every time we passed another family member, we did a double high five. We kept the ritual for about a month's time, and it felt great to connect in this way. Taking those few seconds to become aware of the other person's presence changed the energy of our space. I invite you, just for today, to connect in some way each time you pass a family member. Maybe you would like to do a double high five, a hug, or create your own way of connecting with that person and becoming more aware of their presence.

To cultivate your own awareness, observe yourself and your actions, but resist the urge to criticize or judge yourself. Become aware of how you handle different situations throughout your day. Aim to be present and mindful as much as possible as you ride the waves of existence.

Become Aware

Mantra to cultivate awareness- So-Hum (Sanskrit for I am or nothingness). I am here.

Sit and focus on your breath while repeating the mantra to yourself, either aloud or in your mind. Start with a few and try to build up to 108 repetitions, which is the traditional number of times a mantra is repeated in Japa meditation. If you have a mala, meditation necklace, you can use it to keep count of your repetitions.

Welcome Joy

What brings you joy? What lights you up from the inside out? To my ears, there is no better sound than a baby laughing while experiencing pure joy. Their whole being lights up, and they embrace joy easily. I also get immense joy from watching my children treat each other with kindness, and the wonderful moments when everything aligns beautifully.

When is the last time you allowed yourself to be immersed in joy? To let it all go and laugh, dance, and smile from ear to ear?

Taking just a few moments a day to make joy your priority can shift your perspective greatly. We are here to enjoy life and cherish the good.

Dance for Joy

Have a dance party with your family, or do something you love with your whole heart. Let it all go! That is your work for today!

Practice Non-Harm - Ahimsa

The yogic principle of ahimsa means non-violence towards all living things, non-harm.

We all have that inner voice of constant chatter in our minds and practicing mindfulness quiets it. What does your inner voice say? Are you kind to yourself and others or do unkind thoughts creep in more than you would like them to?

We are all human, and we are all here to learn. Maybe you lost your temper and yelled at your child. Maybe you feel guilty and ashamed for having done so, and you want to beat yourself up. You can apologize to your child, and they will easily forgive you. Can you offer that same grace to yourself? Ahimsa means not allowing yourself to hold onto anger toward yourself. It means speaking to yourself with the same love and kindness that you offer to others.

It is said that how you do one thing is how you do everything. In yoga asana, you can push yourself to your edge without overdoing it and causing harm. You find the place of balance between growth and destruction, too much effort and not enough. This is ahimsa.

Welcome Kindness
Legs-up-the-Wall Pose-Viparita Karani

To perform this passive inversion, start seated on the floor with your right shoulder, hip, and thigh against a wall. Extend arms out to the sides or out in goal posts. You may want a small pillow for resting your head. Relax.

When ready to release from the posture, lower your legs and roll to the right side then use your hand to press yourself back up to sitting.

Practicing this posture is a great way to remember to be kind to yourself.

Remember to Pause

As mothers, our days are always busy. We are serving others in a variety of ways, filling our lives with action. We change diapers, kiss boo-boos, feed hungry children, wash dirty dishes, do laundry, give hugs, drive to activities, and so much more.

I invite you to pause. Take a deep breath and be present with it all. Savor the moment that is now.

Have you ever had a conversation with an older woman where she tells you to treasure every moment because before you know it your children will be grown? I seem to be receiving this wisdom a lot lately, and it serves as a reminder for me to take mini-breaks throughout the day, to savor the present.

For today, any time you find yourself just going through the motions, try to pause and take a deep breath. By cultivating that awareness, you will have given yourself the gift of pause.

Do you feel different when you take time to be in the now?

Invite Contentment

Are you familiar with the song from The Little Mermaid where she expresses that although she has so much stuff, she wants more? She wants legs to walk on land. She believes life will be better for her out of the sea.

Our society seems always to be sending the message that we need to have more, lose 10 pounds, drive a new car, or live in a bigger house, to be happy. Do you internalize these messages? Is there a more fulfilling way of being? How would it look if you practiced contentment and gave thanks for and valued what you already have?

count your blessings
tell yourself you are enough
appreciate what you have
live in the now, not the when

Make a List

Can you think of a few more examples of practices you can incorporate into your being so that your contentment increases? Write them down and look at them whenever you need a reminder of the goodness you are surrounded by.

Practice Self-Discipline - Tapas

Tapas is self-discipline and practicing it helps you "burn off" anything that doesn't serve you. Tapas calls for presence and helps you move forward. In Sanskrit, 'tap' means to heat or cleanse.

Tapas is the process of inner cleansing; we remove things that we do not need.

Do you carry around thoughts that don't serve you? How would it feel if you released them from your being?

Set Them Free

Write down three thoughts you have that do not serve you. Honor them, then release them. Crumble up the paper, rip it, burn it, whatever you need to do to set those thoughts free.

Pillar 4- Food for the Soul

We were all sitting around the dining table one Friday evening eating our dinner. On Friday nights, we light candles, bless the children, and eat a special meal. My youngest son asked me, "What are the ingredients in the food?" I list the ingredients, "Potatoes, broccoli, beef, onions, etc.," and add on to the end, "love."

He looked confused for a minute and said, "Love isn't an ingredient. There is no love in this food." I replied, "Of course there is, sweetheart, love is the special ingredient in all the food I prepare. It's what makes it taste so good and it is why you are so healthy and strong. What do you think you are made of?"

"I don't know," he said. "Love," I told him. "I'm not made of love," he insisted looking very confused. "Of course, you are, it is why you are so sweet," I told him, and a huge smile lit up his entire face as he continued to eat his food.

Honestly, though, love is the secret ingredient in the food I prepare as well as in life. When preparing food, I do so with my entire being, and I pour love into it. It is an expression of my love for myself and my children because we are what we eat. We are made up of the foods we nourish our bodies with, and when we add love and intention to the process, everyone can feel it in the food.

The recipes I am sharing with you are favorites in my home, and I hope you enjoy them. You may notice they are free from some of the top allergens, and that is because we have food allergies in our family. But don't fret, these foods are delicious and nourishing, even without those ingredients included.

Juices

Drinking freshly prepared juice is such a fun and great way to pack in extra vitamins and minerals. I was gifted a juicer by a dear friend, but before I had one, I would make juice in the Vitamix and strain it before serving. You can always serve it as a smoothie and skip the straining part.

Sunrise Juice

This juice will get you out of bed in the morning with a smile. It is filled with life-giving energy, and its sweet flavor will stimulate feelings of joy and contentment.

Ingredients

1/2 mango

6 tangerines

5 strawberries

Juice or blend together and wake up to life. Drink 30 minutes before consuming anything else. Enjoy!

Sarah's Favorite Green Juice

This green juice is bright and refreshing. I find it to be a wonderful way to perk me up in the morning and get my day off to a good start.

Ingredients

1 medium to large sized cucumber

3 apples of your choice (I like granny smiths)

4 stalks celery

1 cup chopped kale

1 lime or 2 key limes

1 inch chunk of ginger (peeled or unpeeled is fine)

Chop the cucumber, apples, celery, and kale into small enough pieces to juice.

Chop the lime and the ginger.

Juice and drink right way. Wake up to the day!

Smoothies

Who doesn't love an aromatic, creamy, cold smoothie? Smoothies are another great way to pack in extra nutrients in a fun and drinkable way.

Berry Green Smoothie

Here is a green twist on a classic berry and banana smoothie. You can add more spinach if you and your children like the taste of it this way. Play with switching up the ingredients. If you prefer kale, go for it! Allow your children to help you with the prep and have fun!

Ingredients
1 cup fresh spinach leaves
2 cups coconut water or non-dairy milk of choice
1 cup blueberries
1 cup strawberries
2 frozen bananas

Blend the spinach and coconut water/milk until smooth.

Add in the blueberries, strawberries, and bananas and blend again until smooth.

Heart Beet Smoothie

Beets are so good for us; they replenish our blood to make us feel healthy and strong. This smoothie is so yummy and just sweet enough to taste like a slice of red velvet cake. And it is dark pink, so it resembles it, too.

Ingredients
2 cups spinach leaves
2 cups unsweetened coconut milk
2 cups frozen strawberries
4 pitted dates
1/4 cup peeled and chopped raw or cooked beets
1 tablespoon cacao powder

Blend the spinach and coconut milk until smooth.
Add the strawberries, dates, beets, and cacao powder and blend again until smooth.
Enjoy!

Breakfast

Starting out the day with some nutrient-dense food gets us off to a good start, both mentally and physically. We have the nutrition we need to concentrate and the energy to get our body moving.

Chickpea Omelette

Makes 1 Omelette (I make 2 to feed my family of 6)

We have food allergies in our family, so the traditional egg omelette is not an option for us. Even if you do eat eggs, this vegan chickpea version is so good, you may even prefer it.

Ingredients

1 tablespoon ground chia + 3 tablespoons water

1 cup chickpea flour

2 tablespoons nutritional yeast

1 teaspoon salt

1/2 teaspoon black pepper

1/2 teaspoon garlic powder

1/2 teaspoon onion powder

1/2 teaspoon turmeric

1/2 cup chopped leafy green of choice (kale, spinach, arugula etc.)

1 cup water

2 tablespoons coconut oil for the pan

In a large mixing bowl, whisk together ground chia and water and let stand until thickened.

Add chickpea flour, nutritional yeast, salt, black

pepper, garlic powder, onion powder, and turmeric.

Whisk in water 1/4 cup at a time until all water is incorporated and no lumps remain. Stir in the chopped leafy greens then set aside to thicken.

Preheat a medium-sized pan over medium heat. Add the oil to the pan and swirl around to coat.

Pour in the batter and cover to cook for 10 minutes. Once the middle of the omelette looks bread-like, flip to cook the other side. Cook this side uncovered for about 8 minutes, or until golden.

Flip onto a plate and enjoy!

Quinoa Muffins

Makes 12 Muffins

Next time you are preparing quinoa, cook up some extra, so you have enough left over to make these delicious and nutrient-dense muffins.

Ingredients

1 cup non-dairy milk of choice (I use unsweetened vanilla coconut milk)

1 tablespoon ground chia seeds

1/4 cup coconut oil

1/4 cup pure maple syrup or agave nectar

1/2 teaspoon vanilla extract

1 1/2 cups flour of choice (we are gluten-free so I use 1 1/4 cups of sorghum/teff flour blend with 1/4 cup arrowroot starch)

1 1/2 teaspoons baking powder

1/2 teaspoon salt

1 teaspoon ground cinnamon

1 1/4 cups cooked quinoa

1/2 cup dried apricots (or dried fruit of choice)

Preheat the oven to 350 degrees and lightly grease a 12-cup muffin tin.

In a medium-size bowl, whisk together the coconut milk and ground chia seed. Allow to sit for a few minutes, then whisk in coconut oil, maple syrup, and vanilla.

In a separate large bowl, sift together flour, baking soda, baking powder, salt, and cinnamon. Add the wet ingredients to the dry, mixing until just incorporated. Gently fold in the cooked quinoa and the apricots and mix until the large clumps are gone.

Pour into the prepared muffin tin and bake for 20 to 22 minutes until a toothpick inserted into the center of a muffin comes out clean.

Lunch

Quinoa Rainbow Salad

This quick and nutritious lunch is a favorite in my home and a great way to "eat the rainbow."

Ingredients
For the salad:
2 cups cooked quinoa
1 cup cooked chickpeas
1/2 of a red bell pepper diced
1 carrot grated finely
1/2 bunch cilantro chopped
1/2 cup chopped purple cabbage
1/4 cup diced onion

For the dressing:
1/4 cup olive oil
3 tablespoons soy sauce
2 tablespoons rice vinegar
1 tablespoon toasted sesame oil
2 teaspoons honey or maple syrup
1 clove of garlic minced or grated
Grated fresh ginger to taste

You may have extra dressing depending on how saucy you like your food. Enjoy over a bed of mixed greens or on its own with a side of fruit.

Romaine Boats

My children came up with this simple and fun way to eat lunch. They love trying new combinations.

Ingredients

1 head of romaine lettuce

Fillings of choice

We like:

Sunflower butter with raisins (bugs in a rug) or fresh berries

Tuna salad

Tahini and carrot / celery / pepper sticks

Have fun with this one!

Dinner

Wild Rice and Roasted Vegetables (Serves 4-6)

Ingredients

2 cups wild rice

5 cups water

salt to taste

vegetables of your choice for roasting (brussell sprouts, bell peppers, cabbage, eggplant)

Wild rice is earthy and full of vitamins and minerals. I like to add salt to it as it boils because salt releases natural and hidden flavors. I've found that roasted brussels sprouts, cabbage, bell peppers, and eggplant go best with the flavor of the rice.

Prepare the wild rice

Rinse the rice in a strainer under running water. Shake dry.

Place the rice and water in a medium size saucepan and bring to a boil.

Add the salt.

When the water has reached a boil, lower the heat to maintain a simmer, and cover the pan.

Cook at a simmer for 45 minutes.

Check the rice. It should be chewy and some of the grains will have burst open.

You may need to add more time or water in order for all the grains to be tender.

Roast your favorite vegetables at 375 degrees with the oil of your choice and salt and pepper.

Check the vegetables after 20 minutes, mix them around, and add more time as needed (most likely another 10-15 minutes).

Serve the vegetables over the rice and enjoy!

Sweet Potato Curry with Basmati Rice

Creamy, nutrient dense and delicious. My children love to sprinkle the seeds and cilantro on their food. The more they are involved, the more likely they are to eat the food and enjoy it.

Ingredients

2 cups white basmati rice

4 cups water

1 tablespoon oil (I use coconut, and olive is also a good choice)

2 shallots, thinly sliced

2 sweet potatoes, peeled and cubed

3-4 cups fresh baby spinach

2-3 tablespoons red curry paste

1 14-ounce can regular coconut milk

1/2 to 1 cup broth or water

1/2 cup chopped sunflower seeds and cilantro

Prepare the rice.

Rinse the rice in a strainer under running water. Shake dry.

Place the rice and water in a medium size saucepan and bring to a boil.

When the water has reached a boil, lower the heat to maintain a simmer, and cover the pan.

Cook at a simmer for 15-20 minutes or until all water is absorbed.

Prepare the curry.

Heat the oil over medium-high heat. Add the shallots and stir-fry until soft and fragrant. Add the sweet potatoes and stir to coat with oil. Add the curry paste and stir until well-combined.

Add the coconut milk and broth and let it simmer over low heat for 10-15 minutes until thickened. Stir in the spinach until wilted.

Add half of the sunflower seed / cilantro mixture; reserve the rest for topping.

Serve over rice, topped with remaining sunflower seeds / cilantro.

Dessert

Chocolate Cake (gluten-free and vegan) with Chocolate Buttercream Frosting

Even if you don't eat a gluten-free or vegan diet, this cake is so good you won't miss the usual ingredients.

Makes 1 cake in an 8x8 baking dish

Ingredients

3/4 rounded cup sorghum flour

3/4 rounded cup arrowroot starch

1/2 cup unsweetened cocoa powder

1 cup organic coconut sugar

1/2 teaspoon sea salt

1 teaspoon baking powder

1 teaspoon baking soda

1 teaspoon guar gum

1 cup non-dairy milk of choice (I use unsweetened vanilla coconut)

1 chia egg (1 tablespoon ground chia combined with water to equal to 1/4 cup liquid)

3 tablespoons organic coconut oil

2 teaspoons bourbon vanilla extract

1 teaspoon rice vinegar

Preheat the oven to 350 degrees.

Whisk together all dry ingredients.

Add the milk, chia egg, oil, vanilla, and vinegar. Mix the batter for a full two to three minutes until all the ingredients are incorporated, and the batter is smooth.

Bake in the center of a preheated oven for 25 minutes or until a toothpick inserted in the center comes out clean.

Cool the cake on a wire rack.

Chocolate Buttercream Frosting (vegan)

1 cup cocoa powder, unsweetened (sifted)

1 1/4 sticks of vegan butter (softened)

3 1/2 cups powdered sugar, organic (sifted)

1/2 cup non-dairy milk (room temperature)

1 tsp vanilla extract

Add the butter, milk, vanilla extract and cocoa powder to a large mixing bowl and using a fork, mash them together until the liquids thicken with the fluffy cocoa.

Add the powdered sugar one cup at a time and mix until fluffy. Do not over mix the frosting to avoid melting the vegan butter too much.

Ice the cake and enjoy!

Chickpea Chocolate Chip Cookies

Ingredients

1½ cups cooked chickpeas

½ cup sunflower butter, or nut butter of your choice

3 tablespoons chickpea flour

3 tablespoons coconut sugar

2 tablespoons maple syrup

2 tablespoons coconut oil

2 teaspoons vanilla extract

¼ teaspoon baking soda

¼ teaspoon baking powder

½ teaspoon salt

½ cup chocolate chips

Preheat the oven to 350 degrees. Grease a baking sheet or line it with parchment paper.

Place the ingredients (except the chocolate chips) in the blender and blend until smooth. Transfer the batter to a bowl and fold in the chocolate chips.

Scoop a heaping tablespoon of batter onto the baking sheet. Repeat until all the batter is used.

Bake for 18-20 minutes, until the edges of the cookies are slightly firm. Let the cookies cool completely (they'll firm up as they cool) before enjoying.

Part III

Chapter 5

Rock Your Ruby Slippers, Lovely

"Today You Are You, That Is Truer than True. There Is No One Alive Who Is Youer than You!" – Dr. Seuss

You are an amazing and magnificent being, the only you there ever was and will be. The sperm that created you, won! Many others were trying to win the race, but you were the one that needed to come.

Yes, some moments and days are more challenging than others, but you've got this. And when things get really crazy, call on your support sisters, and they will remind you how amazing you are.

If that even feels like too much, scream, cry, read a book, watch a movie, move your body, or do whatever it takes to release what's keeping you down. Please, don't hold it in or feel like you need to carry the weight of the world on your shoulders. It simply isn't your responsibility.

Do what makes you feel alive! Paint, play with your children, laugh until it's hard to catch your breath. Remember you are pure love. Shower yourself with the same love you give to others. We are all walking the path of motherhood together. What's good for you, is good for us all. Women united can change the world and make it a place filled with love. Our healing is the drop in the water that will create a ripple effect to healing those around us.

Honoring Self

Your intuition is the only authority worth listening to. You don't need anyone's approval but your own, and the answers you seek are always within you.

Sometimes, the answers we seek may appear to be elusive, but they are always available if we search for them. When you have a question or doubt about something, take a few deep breaths and ask yourself the questions you have. Notice any shifts in your body. Did one option feel more expansive and "right?" There is your answer. Our bodies know what our minds sometimes fail to see.

Getting in touch with your essence allows you to have more self-confidence and feel good about the choices you make. I am including a guided meditation for you to meet and connect with your essence, the pure love within you. If there is someone who can read this aloud to you, that is ideal. Or maybe you can make a voice recording and listen to it. If not, stay as relaxed as you can while reading through it and you will still receive the same benefits.

The Wise Woman Within-Guided Visualization for Revealing your Essence

Begin by finding a comfortable place to sit or lie.

Now inhale and exhale deeply and slowly, bringing your awareness to your breath.

You will now relax every part of your body, beginning with your toes. Tense your toes, and release and relax them.

Now do the same with your entire foot.

Your ankles.

Your calves.

Your knees.

Your entire lower leg.

Your thighs.

Your hips.

Your entire upper leg.

Your back.

Your shoulders.

The back of your torso.

Your abdomen.

Your chest.

The front of your torso.

Your fingers.

Your hands.

Your arms.

Tense and release your neck.

Your jaw.

Your entire face.

Your head.

You are relaxed from head to toe.

I invite you now to picture yourself in a beautiful place in nature. It can be someplace you have already been or a place you would like to go, perhaps by a body of water, in the woods, or on a mountain.

Because it is someplace you love being, you feel very safe there.

You see a path up ahead and decide to explore where

it goes. You discover it leads to a secret garden that is surrounded by a gate.

You find the entrance and open the door and enter the garden.

You look through the garden and see a wise woman sitting

among the flowers waiting to greet you.

You hug her, feel the love she has, filling you up, and she invites you to sit with her.

You feel so good in her presence and decide to ask her a question about something that is challenging you right now. (Take as much time as you need to come up with your question, and ask when you are ready.)

You ask your question and you listen carefully as she shares her wisdom with you.

Her response makes you feel as if she knows you intimately, and you are pleased.

You hug the wise woman goodbye, thanking her for the time you shared.

You exit the secret garden and walk back down the path to your sacred place.

You sit down to incorporate the new information you have learned, and you feel the energy coming back into your toes.

Your feet.

Your entire lower leg.

Your thighs.

Your hips.

Your entire upper leg.

Your back.

Your shoulders.

The back of your torso.

Your abdomen.

Your chest.

The front of your torso.

Your fingers.

Your hands.

Your arms.

Your neck.

Your jaw.

Your entire face.

Your head.

You are back in your body with full energy from head to toe.

You take a moment here then open your eyes.

You have the answer you need within you, now and always.

The wise woman is your innate knowing, and it's available to you whenever you call to her.

The Importance of Sisterhood

"I'm having one of those days," I tell my sister-friend on the phone. "I miss my mom, my heart hurts, and I'm yelling at my children more than I would like to." Even saying the words makes me feel a little better.

"It's ok," she replies. "Can you take a minute for yourself and go have a good cry? Nobody expects you to be perfect and your children always forgive you. They love you, and everything will shift. Nothing stays the same forever," she reminds me.

"You are right. I am so deep in the sadness and anger; I am not sure how I will get out of it. And I feel awful because the words coming out of my mouth are harsh," I tell her.

"Take a deep breath," she instructs me.

"OK, did it," I tell her. "I feel lighter already."

"What is the next best thing for you to do now?" she asks.

As the tears roll down my face, I already have my answer. "I'm crying, and it feels so good," I tell her. "Thanks so much for reminding me that letting go is easier than holding on to it all. I appreciate you and our friendship."

Do you have a friend that you can call no matter what and at any time? One who knows you in and out and holds you in love? If so, treasure her. If you are seeking a sister-friend, tell the universe. Magical things happen when we are open to receive them.

Sisterhood Circle

The value of having a group of women to support and celebrate with you is immeasurable. If you have a close group of sister-friends, treasure them. If there are women's circles taking place in your area, attend if you can.

I hope the words within these pages have empowered and inspired you. The path and practice of motherhood is sacred and the realities of it universal. We share the deepest fears and the strongest love as we mother the next generation. I honor you, incredible woman, and it's my pleasure to share my work with you.

Bibliography

Allrich, Karina. "Gluten-Free Goddess Recipes." Gluten-Free Goddess Recipes, 2 Dec. 2018, glutenfreegoddess. blogspot.com/.

Byrne, Rhonda. The Power. Kosmos, 2010.

Collins, Elise Marie. Chakra Tonics. Red Wheel, 2006.

Godofsky, Ilene. "Vegan & Gluten-Free Recipe Blog." The Colorful Kitchen, 3 Apr. 2017, thecolorfulkitchen. com/.

Hansard, Jen, and Jadah Sellner. Simple Green Smoothies: 100 Tasty Recipes to Lose Weight, Gain Energy, and Feel Great in Your Body. Rodale, 2016.

Krucoff, Carol. Yoga Sparks: 108 Easy Practices for Stress Relief in a Minute or Less. New Harbinger Publications, Inc., 2013.

McClure, Vimala Schneider. The Tao of Motherhood. New World Library, 2011.

Mesko, Sabrina. Healing Mudras: Yoga for Your Hands. Mudra Hands Publishing, 2013.

Millman, Dan. Way of the Peaceful Warrior: a Book That Changes Lives. Kramer, 1984.

Ostrum, Lindsay. "A Food Blog with Simple and Tasty Recipes." Pinch of Yum, 11 Jan. 2016, pinchofyum.com/.

Page, Joseph Le, and Lilian Le Page. Yoga Toolbox for Teachers and Students: Yoga Posture Cards for Integrating Mind, Body & Spirit: a Powerful Tool for Healing. Integrative Yoga Therapy, 2005.

Roy, Denise. Momfulness: Mothering with Mindfulness, Compassion, and Grace. Jossey-Bass, 2007.

Tsabary, Shefali. Awakened Family: How to Raise Empowered, Resilient, and Conscious Children. Penguin Books, 2017.

Tsabary, Shefali. The Conscious Parent. Penguin Books, 2014.

About the Author

Sarah holds a Master's Degree in Social Work from the University of Maryland, Baltimore and she has completed two Yoga Teacher trainings. One in hatha yoga, the other in prenatal yoga. She is also a certified Yoga Birth Instructor. She was a Peace Corps volunteer in the Dominican Republic. She is the mother of five beautiful children who are her greatest teachers.

Sarah combines her social work skills, yogic philosophy, and nature's wisdom to help moms connect with their inner knowing and celebrate their role as a mother. She believes that there will always be a laundry pile waiting to be folded, and that life and motherhood are to be enjoyed, peaks and valleys and all.

Made in the USA
Middletown, DE
19 September 2019